INSPIRATION, FOCUS AND MENTAL FREEDOM.

The Tools Are Here

Are you stuck wondering when your time to shine will come? Are you tired of competing *against* yourself? Are you struggling with purpose as a gymnast?

No matter what you define as success, each gymnast has a dream of becoming a great athlete.

In this practical, easy to understand and action-oriented book, Amy Twiggs, Owner and Director of Flippin' Awesome Gymnastics, will help you apply proven methods to become a leader in the gym. Twiggs has personally used every piece of information in this book herself for many years in her successful career.

> *Twiggs explains, "As a former competitive gymnast, I've been there; I know what it feels like to try your best and to fail. I also know how it feels to work hard to achieve your goals. I remember being a beginner gymnast watching the elites perform and deciding that I wanted to compete at that same level someday."*

Flippin Awesome Gymnast Vol. III reveals a proven approach to becoming the successful and inspirational gymnast you desire to be.

In this how-to guide, the reader will be given tools to:

- Clearly see what judges look for in top performances
- Ensure recognition from coaches and empower your workouts
- Change your perspective during both trials and triumphs at the gym
- Become an amazing and influential gymnast for others to emulate

No matter your current ability, whether you feel like you have little talent or are capable of so much more, know that by following the information in *Flippin' Awesome Gymnast Vol. III,* you will **become an inspiring gymnast**.

Don't let your time as a gymnast keep slipping away; take it back, make it productive, and enjoy your new gymnastics life.

What you're becoming is more important than what you're accomplishing as a gymnast.

Making no change to your daily gymnastics routine is like living your past presently.

It's time to pass Level 1.   **3-2-1 Go!**

FLIPPIN' AWESOME GYMNAST

Vol. III

5 Tools to Become An Inspiring Gymnast

Amy Twiggs

ISBN-13: 978-1-949015-065

TABLE OF CONTENTS

Dedication

I would like to dedicate this book to the following people:

MY PARENTS

They have always been my greatest fans. Their dedication to my personal and athletic success continues to inspire me. I'm continually grateful for their guidance and unconditional love.

MY HUSBAND, TYLER

He has supported my efforts to strive to become someone better than I was yesterday. His patience and sacrifice on my behalf is endearing and appreciated.

FOUR WONDERFUL TEENAGERS

Every day, I get to learn from my teenagers. They are each unique. However, together, they make an entertaining and dynamic team. Much of my joy comes from being near these amazing youths.

Every gymnast, coach and team I have had the pleasure of working with, thank you!

AND ALL OF YOU WHO ARE READING THIS BOOK
-THANK YOU-

INTRODUCTION

Unlike many sports, gymnastics is individually focused. Team synergy is not typically developed along the road to gymnastics success. Although there are team awards throughout the competitive years of this sport, the emphasis is on the individual.

However, a key path to finding a deeper passion and higher purpose during your gymnastics career includes looking outside your own daily success and building those around you. Becoming a team player in an individually centered sport will grant you a sense of constant direction and leadership opportunities.

When is the last time you've noticed another gymnast's success and felt joy for and praised that teammate? When have you chosen to thank a coach who has spent hours of unrecognized work on behalf of your success?

This book helps you recognize and remember your innate desire to contribute to the world. You will find reasons to notice those around you who've helped you realize that you were good enough, strong enough, and brave enough to attempt skills you once thought impossible. *Flippin' Awesome Gymnast, Volume III* has been designed to uncover the hidden leadership talents within you.

This book provides strategies to overcome limiting beliefs that affect your personal fulfillment as a gymnast. As a former gymnast for over 15 years, I know what it feels like to stay in the background, silently obey direction from others, and hide emotions in hopes of realizing potential.

I understand the feelings of losing the joy of gymnastics. I've had the desire to quit the sport when skills got hard. And I've also felt concern regarding the question, "Who am I without gymnastics?" Gymnasts and many others who suffer from emotional insecurities and mental blocks have experienced great success by utilizing the tips found in this helpful guide to becoming an inspiring gymnast.

Abby, a former gymnast from Sacramento, CA says, "The best thing about this book is that it helped me have more confidence in myself. I understand now that I can make a difference in the lives of those around me as I work to make my own life better!"

I promise that if you implement the five simple tools found in this book, you'll immediately see and feel an increased excitement for gymnastics, be more willing to improve yourself from the inside out, and find a focused purpose to help others around you succeed. Don't be the person who misses this opportunity in your athletic life because you believed gymnastics to be just about you.

Be the person others look to for inspiration. Be the kind of person others look at and say, "I want to be like you!" Be the kind of person who makes a change in your life today and takes some action right now. The quick tools you're about to learn have been used by many to create positive personal leadership qualities.

All you have to do is take each step one at a time, continue to read, and begin applying these simple principles today. Each lesson will give you a new tip to become the gymnast others aspire to emulate. Decide now to take a step up to a higher level of gymnastic performance than you've ever imagined.

3-2-1, Go!

My Story:

"Don't be afraid if things seem difficult in the beginning. That's only the initial impression. The important thing is not to retreat; you have to master yourself."

—Olga Korbut

"There's no situation that will ever have power over you if you know who you are. Knowing who you are will change what you want.
Knowing what you want will change what you believe. Knowing what you believe creates a future of limitless possibilities!"

—Amy Twiggs

My elite routine began to develop when I was in kindergarten. I started gymnastics at the age of eight. Whether I was at the gym or watching the Olympics, I found myself intently observing higher-level gymnasts perform tricks that looked exhilarating. I was constantly imagining myself doing those same skills. Gymnastics became a part of my soul. It was woven into the fabric of my life. There was no separating gymnastics from me.

Just like any enthusiastic young gymnast, you would find me doing handstands and practicing the next skill outside our home on the grass or on the metal bars at my elementary school after the last bell rang. I recall ripping off a large part of the skin on my palm in the process of learning skills on those metal bars. What was a little flesh wound in exchange for feeling the rhythm of a bar kip as I would pop my body up onto the bar?

(A bar kip is a movement on the uneven parallel bars in which you glide your body under the bar, extend fully, and then pull yourself to a resting position with your stomach on the bar.)

In 3rd grade, I recall an elderly teacher with red curly hair who saw me working aerials, a maneuver in which you perform a cartwheel with no hands touching the ground. I was using the edge of the sidewalk outside this teacher's classroom door to practice. Instead of telling me to stop, she encouraged me to keep trying. I executed my first true aerial in front of that teacher and received an applause to boot.

At that time in my gymnastics career, I knew nothing about the importance of nutrition, sleep, and mental toughness; I just knew that I enjoyed flipping.

By the age of 15, I had progressed considerably as a gymnast. The Junior Olympics, or J.O., gymnastics program starts at level 1, progresses to level 10, and ends at Elite as the highest level. Level 10 and Elite gymnasts compete at college or in the Olympics. Typically, a competitive gymnast begins at level 3 then works through each level until they qualify for Elite.

During my club gymnastics years, I trained with the Arizona Twisters. At that time, Arizona Twisters didn't compete at level 10. Instead, the gymnasts would try out for elite after level 9. This was a legal and common path for many higher-level gymnasts at that time. I had attended two Elite qualification meets with two teammates, both of whom had reached the qualifying score on their first try, but I had not. They still came to the other qualifying meets just for more experience.

I didn't know it at the time, but my parents had purchased a necklace for me with my name and the word "elite" engraved on it, which they planned to give to me after the first qualifying meet. When I did finally qualify for elite after the third meet, my parents presented me with the necklace and I inquired about it. My dad told me he and my mom both knew I would become an elite eventually; there was no question in their minds. They knew it just like I did.

Failing at my first two attempts didn't discourage me from working a little harder to make my routines just a little better in order to progress further in the sport. This is the nature of gymnastics.

I currently love the song, "Get Back Up Again" from the movie, Trolls. To me, this is the perfect theme song for a gymnast's life. Every day, we fall in practice over and over, but we learn from day one of gymnastics that you always get back up again. There's no holding a gymnast down for long. Lingering in self-pity on the ground doesn't serve any gymnast well.

Around this same age, I was taught positive affirmations and visualization techniques by my older brother during the summer he spent home from college. These tools, along with relaxation and breathing techniques, became a consistent part of my daily routine. I attribute much of my confidence and success as an elite gymnast to those four tools.

At the age of 16, I experienced a kind of out-of-body episode because I had practiced visualization in such detail every night before I fell asleep. At that time, I was preparing for a national team qualifying competition that was to take place at the Delta Center in Salt Lake City, Utah.

For six months prior to that competition, I had daily visualized the eight routines I was to perform. One tumbling pass, in particular, had caused me some anxiety in practice, but no longer held any power over me due to the visualization technique. Upon landing that tumbling pass at the competition, I experienced dèjá vu in a way I had never before felt it. The details of my routines were all performed precisely as I had envisioned them to be.

Although I had never actually been in the Delta Center, the arena layout, equipment set up, and general audience were everything I had imagined in my mind they would be. For a brief moment, I wasn't sure if I were in my bed at home visualizing this pass or actually performing at the arena.

Instantly, I knew there was power in the thoughts I had created in my mind and the words I had chosen to believe. It was beyond my ability to clearly explain. Since that experience at the Delta Center, I have used those same tools to adapt and refine my daily routine to become the person I am today.

I obtained a full-ride women's gymnastics scholarship and received a Psychology Degree from Stanford University. I am now a wife to an amazing man and a mother of four teenagers. I also own a gymnastics company, Flippin' Awesome Gymnastics, where I love to continually serve gymnasts.

My daily routine from the age of 15 to the present and in the future will continue to progress as I learn, understand, and gain more knowledge and life experience.

High-performing athletes often hear comments such as, "I don't know how you do all you do" or "Why do you want to do all that?" or "You should just sit and relax more often" or "I could never do what you do." Many people are astonished by the intense regimens that elite athletes choose.

Anyone can live an elite lifestyle if they choose to. Motive and desire are keys to any change. If you're reading this book, then chances are you have a desire to make changes to your current athletic routine.

I am offering athletic techniques that are applicable to everyone. If utilized, these tools will get you to a more impactful level of daily performance. This book will inspire greatness, increase confidence, and crush fears.

When you create your moments, days, dreams, and life, you're living intentionally. Do those hard things, make those uncomfortable choices, surprise yourself by exposing your own undiscovered capabilities. Elite performers narrow their daily choices to produce unimaginable results.

1
The Sweet Spot

"A Player who makes a team great is better than a great player."

—John Wooden

"Don't waste your time on jealousy. Sometimes you're ahead; sometimes you're behind. The race is long and, in the end, it's only with yourself."

—Mary Schmich

"It's important to push yourself further than you think you can go each and every day — as that is what separates the good from the great."

—Kerri Strugg

CHAPTER 1 TOOLS:

The Sweet Spot

The Sweet Spot is the name of a mat used in gymnastics to give an added boost to a gymnast while tumbling. If you hit the mat right in the center, on the marked bull's-eye, you receive the maximum flight benefit for the skill. As a gymnast, the Sweet Spot can also mean the moments when mental, emotional, and physical abilities synergize to create an inspiring show for all who get to be a part of and watch it.

In most sports, athletes are working for a specific future goal. Once that goal is attained, then the process repeats. Practice, work, rhythm, diet, sleep, mental work, compete, again, again. This routine continues until, finally, you come to an endpoint in your game.

One tool I want to offer here is the concept that instead of working solely for the next tournament or meet, work to enjoy the present moment or the process of growing in your sport. Your years in any sport are limited. Build yourself as well as your teammates, coaches, and those looking up to you along the way.

When you plan for a vacation, you save, research, and look forward to the entertainment ahead. However, in the end, your final endpoint is actually getting back home. So, why leave home in the first place? You leave for the thrill of the journey, not the final destination.

With gymnastics, your final destination is not just the next meet or the Olympics. If those endpoints were your final destination, then life would be somewhat disappointing. Look forward to these moments, knowing that they won't last long. A gymnast's total performance time at any given meet is less than 10 minutes between all four events. The meets take about three hours to sit through, but the actually show time is minimal.

With this in mind, the worry and stress you place on yourself, based on a future performance that hasn't actually even occurred seems a bit misplaced. If the majority of your sport's experience is in the gym facility, then why not find and feel the excitement in those moments as if every practice were a competition.

If every practice were a performance, then you would always be pushing yourself to do your best; you would always be mentally prepared and physically energized to do more than you thought you could. If you learn to make every moment a destination in your mind, then when it comes time to retire from whatever sport you choose, you'll have thousands of highlights to think back on, instead of just the few judged competitions. When your body is unable to continue performing, your mind will continue enjoying.

Happiness is a choice. Choose happy. Choose it today. It's contagious and will lift those around you. Every moment is a destination. Make your destiny happen intentionally every day. Enjoy the journey. You'll find that the physical portion of your valued sport ends way too quickly, but your mental satisfaction from that sport will never end.

One way you can choose to make every moment a highlight is by working on sharing your talent through developing separator tools. This will give you something to focus on in order to stand out and, in the process, be a leader to your team. Every team needs someone to show them how to put on a true performance.

A separator tool in gymnastics is the difference between a 9.95, 9.975, and a 10.00 score. As a gymnast, you must stand out in your performance at a competition. How do you do this?

For judges, the term is often referred to as *separators.* Separators are those little, minute distinctions that set you apart from your competitor. It can be the difference between a sickle foot in dance or a polished, energetic flick of the finger defining the end of each pose.

This tool helps a judge decide who will take the gold when the routines are equally presented and performed. A judge may decide one routine fit the music better, another's choreography was more aesthetically pleasing, the lines were straighter, or the dynamics were stronger.

It's the energy that a gymnast portrays when bringing movements to life or giving the audience a show instead of just another routine. When the audience gives unsolicited applause for a floor routine because they couldn't help themselves, then you know the routine has something noteworthy.

When the routine is so engaging and entertaining that judges want to be a part of the experience also, then you can know you have done something remarkable and have truly shared your talent.

These are the details that appear as separators to judges. Ask yourself how you can be bold and different from others? What sets you apart from your competitor? Why should a judge give you a better score than the next gymnast? Why do you think you're special as a gymnast?

When reading these questions, your mind may have immediately jumped to one of three points on a spectrum of confidence. The thought popped into your head that, *"Nothing makes me special,"* a self-effacing or insecure idea. On the other extreme is, *"Of course, the judges would choose me because no one is as good as me,"* which is pride or arrogance. Lastly, the healthy middle, well-balanced space is thinking that a judge would choose your routine above another because you know that you're in the zone and ready and it shows every time you get the chance to demonstrate your passion for the sport.

This view of yourself is the perfect confidence spot, or what I like to call the **Sweet Spot**. As I said in the beginning of this chapter, the Sweet Spot mat gives you a boost to the greatest height possible in order for you to perform a skill with less gravitational pull for a brief moment. This is the same for a performance in the daily moments of your life as a gymnast. How can you bring all the pieces together to reach your highest level of performance in the gym?

When you perform in "The Sweet Spot" of your emotions, you're performing from a place of confidence and inner-peace. You're not comparing yourself to the gymnasts around you. You're not engaging in negative self-talk, reminding yourself of all your flaws. You prepare physically and mentally in practice daily, so that when the meet comes, you're successful no matter the outcome.

This emotional sweet spot shines through in your every move. The judges see and feel the energy surrounding you. The score "separators" are easy to recognize when you see a gymnast perform in their Sweet Spot as opposed to a place of self-effacement or pride. Your true identity shines in the competition clearly. Others look to emulate your style, but what they're really trying to find is their own "Sweet Spot."

Next time you perform, or watch a performance, notice the way the top achievers hold themselves. A person in tune with their confident Sweet Spot positively affects everyone around them.

Gymnastics is one of the few sports that doesn't make a game plan against competitors. There's little time spent studying the opposing teams. Every day is a competition against yourself. Or, conversely, every day is an opportunity to rise to the stand.

Look in the mirror to decide who you want to compete against today: your best self or your mediocre self? Whether workouts or competitions, it doesn't matter. You have no competitors to beat except yourself. Every day, is a show of your own personal mindset, physical ability, and emotional strength.

As a former USAG judge, I had the power to score gymnasts in many different areas and abilities. I always enjoyed watching gymnasts perform at their best in competitions. However, I wondered at times whether a nervous gymnast understood the repercussions of the way they **appeared** on the beam. There is a specific deduction that judges take termed *Lack of Sureness.* The judge gets to decide if a gymnast "appears confident" while performing on the beam. This means, you may feel confident performing your routine, but if you don't project that confidence, then a judge can lower your score two tenths.

Two tenths is critical in gymnastics. This is a huge score gap in a competition, which could change the result from 1st place to 4th place. Lack of sureness is subjective, which means it's purely decided on the judge's opinion. If you, the gymnast, knew that by holding your chin up a little higher, pulling your shoulders back a bit, sharpening your movements, keeping your eyes focused, and providing the "appearance of confidence" would increase your score by two tenths, wouldn't you try it?

You may not feel confident, but whether you feel it or not, the appearance is all that matters to a judge. And, the powerful secret is that, as you position your body in a confident manner, your mind will begin to believe that you're confident, and those little thoughts will create a feeling until, eventually, you can say, "I AM CONFIDENT."

You no longer receive a "lack of sureness" deduction, but rather a bonus separator score of beautiful artistry and confidence because you've found your Sweet Spot.

As you apply the Sweet Spot to your own gymnastics, you might want to see what happens when you use it to build your team, your coaches, your entire gym. You'll be the leader to help inspire others.

Have you ever noticed a flock of geese flying in a V formation? When the lead goose gets tired, he falls back to the end of the formation in order to coast and use less energy. The head goose is breaking the wind for the entire group, therefore, exerting the most energy. The group protects the elderly by purposely keeping them in the center of the V lines. This allows the elderly geese to use the draft of the lead geese, but also to be pushed by the geese behind, as an encouragement to keep moving forward.

What about an injured goose? When one goose is injured, a couple other geese fly down with that goose to help until they are able to fly again. Then they set off again, sometimes joining a new group depending on how long it took for the injured bird to heal.

Consider this innate, prewired action of the geese. How does this apply to your gymnastics team? As an athlete, you're in a variety of situations. Sometimes, you're competing individually, while other times, your scores count for an entire team. The result of any performance pushes us up or down.

If you see each team member as a part of a V formation, like the geese, then you can decide to lift those struggling with physical or mental ailments. When one member of the team goes down, you can encourage and lift, which will strengthen the team as a whole. When the current leader of your team fails to continually "break the wind" for you, you can step up and be the leader.

Help lift those around you in every area of your life. Protect your team. Lift your team. Be a leader for your team. Your team will do the same for you when you need it. Show them how to fly together in the Sweet Spot of gymnastics.

Chapter 1 Highlights

- The Sweet Spot is an actual piece of gymnastics equipment with a bullseye to show where a gymnast should punch off to receive the maximum height.

- The Sweet Spot is the moment when the emotional, physical, and mental areas of your gymnastics align to produce something spectacular. When you feel confident, bold, capable, and flawless.

- In the Sweet Spot, your enjoyment of the sport radiates to lift and influence everyone around you.

- Teammates, coaches, and judges enjoy the gift of watching you perform in your Sweet Spot.

- Everyone feels edified because of watching your workouts and performances when you are coming from a place of total harmony within yourself.

- Work to find enjoyment in the process of the daily workouts as you take care of every aspect of your life in order to fly from the center of your own personal sweet spot.

What's Ahead in Chapter 2

Learn to filter what you will and won't allow to come out of your mouth. The words you choose to speak will either increase desire for coaches and others to help you, or they will crush your athletic career quickly.

Chapter 1 Action Items

Journal:

1. How can you be bold and be different from others?
2. What sets you apart from your competitor?
3. Why should a judge give you a better score than the next gymnast?
4. Why do you think you're special as a gymnast?
5. How can you be a leader in your gym for others to want to emulate?
6. How will being confident help your teammates succeed?

2
Words You Never Say

"I don't run away from a challenge because
I am afraid. Instead, I run toward it
because the only way to escape fear is to
trample it beneath your feet."

—Nadia Commanici

"Listening is being able to be changed by
the other person."

—Alan Alda

"Confidence is silent. Insecurities are loud."

—Unknown

CHAPTER 2 TOOLS:

Words You Never Say

"I already know that " and "I can't." These phrases destroy confidence, weaken abilities, and crush dreams.

Growing up, there were few verbalized rules in my home. However, there was one phrase which, if we were caught saying it out loud, we would get a quick reminder from my dad to stop and think about what we just implied. This phrase was, "I can't."

We were always reminded how damaging this was to our progress in anything. Saying, "I can't" assumes you've tried something from every possible angle and there are no solutions left to try. "I can't" tells your brain that you're incapable of finding solutions and, therefore, this skill isn't worth the effort to try.

Today, if I hear a gymnast in my gym say, "I can't," then I, too, stop my class and correct that error immediately. You're always capable of more than you think. There's always another way to solve a problem.

If I hear this phrase, I ask the gymnast to do ten push-ups in order to get more blood flowing to their brains and more strength in their body so they can figure out a solution to their situation.

All of my gymnasts now catch each other and remind the others to keep trying. Don't allow yourself to believe lies. Don't fall victim to quitting because your brain wants to offer you an easy way out. Push on, try again, believe you can do more, then get up and move.

When you feel your mouth wanting to blurt out, "I can't," try "I can." This little change will give you an added measure of desire and energy to go again. We don't know our own limits. The only limits we truly experience are the ones we place on ourselves. See how much more you're capable of doing by saying, "I can!"

Furthermore, some people believe that if they've heard something in the past, then the information is already ingrained in their heads and they no longer need to hear it again. Hal Elrod, author of *The Miracle Morning*, and a motivational speaker, has suggested everyone avoid the phrase, "*I already know that.*" These four words shut down communication, leave you with your own past results, and halt any further progress.

Repetition is valuable to progression. When a gymnast is learning a new skill, a coach may continually remind the gymnast to squeeze, lift, or punch at a precise moment. We need to relearn and repeat actions and words for our body to respond to new directions. Our mind needs repetition as well to create new mental habits.

A few years ago, I was coaching a group of girls who had only a couple weeks left until their high school drill team tryouts. They each needed an aerial cartwheel in order to have a chance at making the team. This limited time put the pressure on them to work hard. Immediately, I got a sense of who would progress with me as their coach.

A couple girls kept eye contact with me every time I suggested a new drill or a strength movement. One athlete came 20 minutes late and stood in a relaxed manner with her hand on her hip when I tried to advise her on how to improve. She finally informed me that what I was asking her to do would make her aerial worse. She felt lighter in the air with her old style.

In essence, she told me that she "already knew" what I was saying wouldn't work for her. I gave her permission to work on her own. She proceeded working on her aerial over and over in a way that did nothing to get her closer to her goal while I focused on coaching the girls who were attempting the ideas provided. Eventually, the solo athlete joined us and asked if I would teach her the new technique and help her as well.

Change doesn't always make things easier or better initially, but oftentimes, it does evolve into something greater. It's just like cleaning out a room. At first, the mess may seem overwhelming, but in the end, the work is well worth the effort. Next time you want to say, "I already know that," try "What else can you teach me?" instead.

These phrases are honestly just a sign of impatience. When you want something to happen fast, and your results aren't apparent, most gymnasts will feel like giving up. Think about this idea: Try keeping your head down at times. What do I mean by "keep your head down"?

After all the confidence blogs, podcasts, and books about holding your head up, this seems to counter all my other advice. As I teach the simple pullover skill on the low bar with over 100 developmental gymnasts weekly, I have realized that a common problem they consistently have is lifting their heads as soon as their hips get on top of the bar. They are responding too quickly to their perceived successful mastery of the skill, .

There is still work to be done before mastering the pullover. As much as I tell them to keep their heads down in order for the body weight to balance over the bar, most fight this advice and lift their heads. The result of lifting your head as soon as your hips are on top of the bar is that your body will fall forward. This frightens some children into listening to my suggestions.

Falling forward is counterproductive and not at all helpful in completing the pullover. Once a gymnast listens and responds to the advice given, they usually find that keeping their heads down while adjusting their body weight over the bar allows for a smooth transition to completion and success of the skill. The gymnast can then finish in a tall, tight, straight arm, stationary, and stable position.

This is applicable to when we want to make a statement such as "I can't" or "I already know that." Sometimes, we get anxious and impatient. We think we should be able to quickly master a skill or know what to do to fix a problem. Or, we assume a circumstance is close enough to completion and we rush on to the next event or task.

Have you noticed that at the end of some movies, there are funny outtake treasures available for those who wait a few extra minutes? When we rush through and think we're done with a skill or an event, we may be missing a treasure that could bring us much joy and a happy surprise.

Think about times when you may have missed an opportunity because you left too early from gym, became a little impatient with a skill, or thought you knew everything and didn't need any more help. A bowed head is a sign of humility. Humility is the desire and ability to seek knowledge, knowing you don't know all.

Instead of lifting your head too quickly in the gym, maybe you should think about keeping your head down at times, and listen to what your coaches are trying to tell you so you can obtain your goals safely and efficiently.

Typically, the underlying emotion for any negative phrase goes beyond impatience, and its root is fear. As an athlete, you must learn to understand fear. It's an emotion that has many minions, including impatience, worry, anxiety, nervousness, distress, disappointment, agitation, alarm, or panic.

Fear has a purpose. We are hard-wired to protect ourselves, and we think that fear keeps us safe to a certain extent. However, when we let fear run our thoughts and choices, then we're very limited in our actions and our results are rarely positive. Most species have a "flight or fight" response, which protects the species from danger.

Humans are capable of another level of fear though, a fear that's only real in our heads. It's a false reality that we create from our thoughts. However, our thoughts are real to us, so they become our reality. When it's dark outside, we may choose to think there are dangers out there that may or may not be real. When we score low at a meet, we may think we're not capable and will never be good enough.

If we allow fear to take over, then our success rate has just plummeted to zero. Everyone experiences fear. Recognize it as an emotion that we all have. It's normal and it has a purpose. Acknowledge that fear is presenting itself. Say hello to your fear. Then, if needed, let fear remain around, while you engage with the emotions that will move you forward. Stop fear from taking over your thoughts right there.

Fear will no longer make you feel stuck or afraid. It's just another emotion hanging around for a visit. The less attention you give it, the less threatening it becomes. Focus on the emotions you want to feel, and, eventually, fear will fade or completely disappear into the background.

When gymnastics seems frustrating, overwhelming, and scary, then try the box idea. Write a list of the things you have control over and can change. Put those written ideas into a box labeled with your name on it. For all the things that come up that you cannot change or don't have control over, write them down as well, but put them into a different box entitled "Universe." Let the universe take care of the situations that you don't know what to do with or how to manage.

You only focus on those things that you can control and you can change. This releases you from many emotions, one of which is fear, and allows you to give the uncontrollable variables away. You only have power to change what's in your control. See what happens to your confidence as you try this exercise.

Marianne Williamson perfectly states a case against fear when she said, "Our deepest fear is not that we are inadequate. Our deepest fear is that we are powerful beyond measure. It is our light, not our darkness that most frightens us. We ask ourselves, "Who am I to be brilliant, gorgeous, talented, and fabulous?" Actually, who are you not to be? You are a child of God. Your playing small does not serve the world. There is nothing enlightened about shrinking so that other people won't feel insecure around you. We are all meant to shine, as children do. We were born to make manifest the glory of God that is within us. It is not just in some of us; it is in everyone and as we let our own light shine, we unconsciously give others permission to do the same. As we are liberated from our own fear; our presence automatically liberates others."

Most competitive athletes have some level of confidence (discussed in Chapter 1), which is the antidote to fear. However, as the competitive levels increase in difficulty, your need to control your thoughts also increases. Your thoughts and words directly influence your level of confidence. Every aspect of sports psychology comes down to the ability of an athlete to have confidence in themselves.

Athletic greatness is all about increasing your confidence. Confidence is trust in yourself and your abilities, whether you're in an individual sport or a team sport. Do you believe you will achieve your goals? Do you believe your team will achieve their goals? Do your teammates want to perform their best as sincerely as you do?

I've heard it said that what you tell yourself is ten times more powerful than what anybody else tells you. It doesn't matter what your coach says, or a sports psychologist, or a best friend. If you tell yourself you will achieve a certain level of success, then your brain will believe you and you will look for opportunities and put in the work to make that happen. When desiring a certain outcome in sports, if you were to take two identical twins, meaning they both had the same capabilities, physical structure, coaching, equal opportunities, and the only difference was that one twin consistently did mental training, then the mentally trained twin would outperform the other twin consistently.

Why? Because being able to manage your thoughts and words creates a reality that's always a success.

This doesn't mean a mentally trained athlete wins every time. This means that win or fail, every opportunity is seen as a success in the sense that the athlete performed better than they did in the past, or is looking forward to learning from what they didn't do.

Managing your mind allows you to fail and see it as an opportunity for growth. There is no failure unless you choose to see it as such. Mental toughness comes from learning from mistakes and getting back up again to work smarter, and to build yourself up in every aspect so you can perform at your peak level.

Therefore, watch what you choose to let slip out of your mouth, search for phrases that will infuse positive outlooks and thoughts in every situation. By doing this, you'll receive motivational help from coaches and others who want to see you succeed.

Chapter 2 Highlights

- Words you never say include phrases such as, "I can't" or "I already know that."

- These types of statements close your mind and body to any further progress in gymnastics. They'll halt progress, stop coaches' help, and decrease motivation.

- You're essentially telling yourself you might as well quit and there's no point in trying.

- Coaches don't want to continue working with gymnasts who incorporate these types of phrases into their athletic careers. Furthermore, you won't want to continue working with yourself. Your confidence becomes shattered as less people interact to your benefit.

- Try using hopeful phrases the next time you find yourself uttering self-destructive phrases.

- Replace "I can't" with "I can" and see what kind of solutions your mind will want to offer you and how your body naturally gives you a little boost.

- Replace "I already know that" with, "What else can you teach me?"

- You may find that your coaches will dig deeper to encourage you and help you on your road to success.

What's Ahead in Chapter 3

If you want to know the secret phrase that will contribute more to you as an athlete than any other tool, then keep reading. This phrase of gratitude gives expected and, often, unexpected positive results as well.

Chapter 2 Action Items

Challenge:

1. Next time you want to say, "I already know that," try "What else can you teach me?" instead!
2. Next time you want to say, "I can't", change it to, "I can," then keep trying.
3. Whenever you want to use a self-destructive phrase, answer this question in your journal: "What am I afraid of?"
4. Once you know what your fears are, then you can understand why you're holding yourself

back. Make a decision to rewrite those phrases by choosing to believe that obstacles are actually opportunities for your own personal growth.

3
Power
Phrase

"No matter what accomplishments you
make, someone helped you."

—Althea Gibson

"Develop an attitude of gratitude, and give
thanks for everything that happens to you,
knowing that every step forward is a step
toward achieving something bigger and
better than your current situation."

—Brian Tracy

CHAPTER 3 TOOLS:

Gratitude

Power Phrase: Thank You!

Law of Attraction: Whatever you put out into the world comes back to you.

Mirroring: Imitating the emotions of others. Positive emotional mirroring reflects your happy emotions intentionally, no matter how others around you behave emotionally. Negative mirroring adopts others' negative emotions and is reactive.

Mirror You: Choosing to see others as you see yourself

Recognizing the help from others in your life will provide greater benefits to you than any other tool that I've been taught as an athlete and can teach you now. Grateful is how we need to wake each morning, live each day, and retire to bed each night. It is the first trait in any worthy and inspiring leader. It requires humility to recognize there's more to life than ourselves. This is true for athletes and it's true for everyone. It has a ripple effect, like a small pebble tossed in a lake. You never know how far your words will reach and then return to your betterment.

Research on the advantages of gratitude is well documented. One such study by Robert A. Emmons and Michael E. McCullough entitled, "Counting Blessings Versus Burdens: An Experimental Investigation of Gratitude and Subjective Well-Being in Daily Life," found that "results suggest that a conscious focus on blessings may have emotional and interpersonal benefits." (*Journal of Personality and Social Psychology,* 2003, vol. 84, no. 2, 377-389, https://greatergood.berkeley.edu/images/application_uploads/Emmons-CountingBlessings.pdf)

These two well-quoted and documented psychologists asked some of their participants to write about topics focused on things they were grateful for, while others were asked to write about their daily disappointments and burdens. They found that those "who wrote about gratitude were more optimistic and felt better about their lives, had fewer visits to the physicians... exhibited a huge increase in happiness scores. This impact was greater than that from any other intervention, with benefits lasting for a month....

Most studies published on this topic support an association between gratitude and an individual's well-being." (Harvard Health Publishing, Harvard Medical School, In Praise of Gratitude, Nov. 2011, https://www.health.harvard.edu/newsletter_article/in-praise-of-gratitude)

Expressing gratitude for any aspect of your life or another's life puts your mind in a humble, teachable state. You're aware of your nothingness and your greatness all in one.

The value of gratitude is one of the many lessons I learned quickly through my early years of gymnastics. The more I said thank you to teachers, mentors, and coaches, the more willing and helpful they seemed to be. I was always grateful when a coach, trainer, or other facilitator would work with me to improve on something with which I was struggling.

During my freshman year at Stanford University, I tore my ACL. I recall limping over to the therapy room and being assessed. The physical trainers determined that I had just sprained my knee and that I would be able to compete at the UC Berkeley meet that weekend. A couple of days before our team was leaving for the meet, I was grateful that a doctor in the athletic facility rechecked my knee.

He immediately stated that my ACL was completely torn and I wouldn't be competing. Instead, he let me know that I would need to have surgery to repair my ACL. I felt no sadness, only gratitude and hope. The team captains came to visit me that night in my dorm room. One captain was in tears over my situation.

I spent the time trying to decide what to say. I didn't want to appear insensitive to the fact that I wouldn't be able to contribute to the team that weekend. However, I had absolute confidence I would heal completely. If this was what I was supposed to experience at that moment in my life, I was at the perfect place to get the best help possible for recovery because Stanford had some of the top-ranked medical doctors. I knew I would be back in top shape and competing the following year.

I felt no fear, no sadness, just gratitude for the entire situation, especially for the power of healing. I appreciated that the senior captains would take time to visit a little freshman. I felt grateful to the Stanford doctor who performed the surgery. I greatly appreciated our gymnastics team athletic trainer, who spent morning and evening attending to my full recovery in preparation for the next season. There are always blessings to be grateful for in every situation.

After 30 years of participating in gymnastics now, I continue to recognize the power of gratitude. My family is the only reason I get to enjoy much of the current blessings of gymnastics in my life. I wouldn't be where I am without the financial and emotional support of my family. For years, my parents and siblings would do paper routes and clean the gym on Saturdays. My mom would sew leotards to sell and was our gym secretary. My parents even decided not to take a great job opportunity in another city because it didn't have higher level gymnastic opportunities for me. Where would I be without them?

There were also many other support systems in place that helped me to excel at the sport such as coaches, friends, family, and doctors. Many helped on my road to becoming an elite gymnast. It's now my turn to give back.

In the Flippin' Awesome Gymnastics facility which I own, my coaches and I start each class with a "focus word." A focus word is a word that we discuss and explain to the gymnasts that can help them with every area of their life, such as Gratitude, Confidence, Hard Work, Patience, Determination, and Leadership.

The focus word for the first month of each session is always Gratitude. We challenge every student to go home and thank their parents for the opportunity to be in their gymnastics class. Enjoying the thank yous coming weekly from three-year-olds softens my heart. These habits created at a young age will provide each child with a powerful edge throughout their lives.

My husband, Tyler, has been a football coach for many years. He helped coach a team that had a dominating season for five years. One football player stood out. He was a natural leader, the one who, no matter what happened at practice or at a game, would thank the coaches.

Tyler once spoke of a game during which this player made a big mistake and was verbally castigated for it.

What impressed Tyler was that after that specific game, this young man went up to each coach and thanked them. It had a great impact on my husband.

When I asked my son, a player on this same team, which teammate he would look to as the leader of the team, he immediately said, "Oh yeah, everyone knows who that is." It just happened to be the same player about whom my husband would often comment.

Whether this quarterback made mistakes and was being strongly reprimanded or doing his job perfectly, he would thank the coaches. My husband immensely enjoyed helping this team. There have been other teams where coaching has been a burden for my husband. In general, this was because of disrespect and ingratitude from the players.

One current method of teaching gratitude is the idea of "mirroring." This typically means that you respond to others in the same way that others act toward you. In other words, you "mirror" what others are portraying. Your energy level or wavelengths, as some call it, are trying to match those of people around you.

If you're experiencing happiness but then are confronted by another person portraying negative emotions, the natural and easy response is to adopt the negative person's emotions as an automatic defense. This kind of mirroring uses the lower brain function.

Ideal "*Mirroring*" means to reflect what you want to see happen, as if you were looking into a mirror and seeing your own reflection when, in reality, you're looking at another person. I will call this the "*Mirror You*." Respond to others as if you're always talking to your best self.

This higher brain functioning is a great way to give back. It requires self-discipline to stay true to yourself. Reacting to another person takes little effort. Working to help ease others' burdens of stress, fear, self-doubt, and anxiety depends upon your own mental game toughness.

How do you respond when a coach gets exasperated with your failures or when a teammate demands another spot when you've been waiting patiently for your own turn? These moments happen often, and if you choose, you could find conflict instead of gratitude in those moments. Use your prefrontal cortex; engage your higher brain abilities and reflect the response you want to enjoy.

Another description of this gratitude idea is expressed as the *Law of Attraction*. This idea simply means that you will receive back, that which you send out into the world. If you react positively to others, then others will react similarly to you. How you treat others is probably how you also treat yourself. In order to use this universal law, the higher brain must be working.

Gratitude also requires greater mental effort. As you intentionally seek for evidence of good in the gym and throughout the day, you will increase your own joy and happiness.

Remember in all of these examples, the most powerful phrase you can say is "thank you." The tool of gratitude applies to every part of life, and especially as an athlete. Today, I continue to use gratitude as the beginning, middle and ending of each day.

Chapter 3 Highlights

- The Power Phrase is saying, "Thank you" as often as possible and see what happens as a result.
- No one ever accomplished greatness on their own.
- There is always someone helping you on your path to glory.
- Recognize those who help.
- Be humble.
- The irrefutable consequence of this habit is powerful, yet, oftentimes, not immediately noticed. Feeling and expressing gratitude is a crucial step on your path to becoming an elite-level athlete.

What's Ahead in Chapter 4

When you're pushing through pain, ignoring the blood on your grips from the hours of bar work, and resisting the tears of disappointment and fear, you can remember something that will always bring you hope: the other side of the Pendulum. This lesson will nudge you to move forward when you want to give up.

Chapter 3 Action Item

Challenge:

Make a greater effort to say thank you to your coaches, teammates, and any others who cross your path today.

4
The
Pendulum

"Be strong when you are weak, brave
when you are scared, and humble when
you are victorious."

—Gabby Douglas

"The cure for pain is in the pain. Good and
bad are mixed, if you don't have both, you
don't belong with us."

—Rumi

The Pendulum is similar to the Newton's Cradle physics toy with metal balls hanging from strings. It symbolizes an emotional swing created by our thoughts in the gym. The idea is that in order to experience joy, you must experience sorrow. Without opposites, choice is gone. Adversity and taking a chance on yourself are requirements for growth and success. A sport is only as meaningful as the struggle directly opposing it.

I went mountain biking with my sister years ago. She was nervous and tight-gripped on her bike. We kept telling her, "keep an eye on what lies ahead as well as on what is right in front of you." She relaxed throughout the ride.

However, on the final stretch of a straight dirt road, she crashed and received some impressive skin rashes and bruises. We asked her about what had happened. She said she found herself enjoying the view, looking too far ahead and not paying attention to what was right in front of her. She had hit a rock without noticing it in advance.

This is often what happens at the gym. As you become more comfortable with your abilities, sometimes, you may lose the perspective of your goals. You might forget the love you felt when you first started gymnastics. Or you look ahead and believe you'll be a collegiate gymnast, yet you skimp on conditioning and come late to gym.

Either way, you miss important pieces to the potential inside of you. When you work hard at a goal and lose sight of why you're working hard, then you eventually burn out and believe that your love for the sport is gone. When you have goals that require patience and consistency, you may become disappointed when the goals aren't reached immediately, thinking you will probably never attain those goals anyway, so why keep trying?

Successful gymnasts find a balance. Daily following the required steps to reach the level of apparent ease and flawlessness of an elite gymnast takes time. Keep a perspective that fills you with hope and excitement. Realize that in order to obtain any goal, you must find a way to enjoy the daily work to get there.

What appears difficult and dangerous to beginning gymnasts, doesn't fill experienced athletes with any fear because of the effort and time they have already invested in the sport. Find a balance between impossible goals and daily doable goals. Eventually, you'll find the impossible is now possible.

I believe positive feelings are in direct correlation, to a certain degree, with negative feelings. Now you must understand that I don't believe we all must encounter every negative experience in life in order to be happy. Luckily, we can learn how to be happy without always experiencing equivalent amounts of sorrow. Thus, we can learn some lessons by observing the mistakes of others.

Have you noticed that we tend to be attracted to stories of people who've experienced great sorrow but, nevertheless, have overcome and triumphed? Those who've suffered and are able to see the good in their experience seem to have a greater sense of compassion and understanding toward others.

As an athlete, I've experienced dislocations, broken ankles, a torn ACL, "mental monkeys" (which are mental fears that debilitate), and other struggles. I felt excitement when my monkeys would go play somewhere else and I could resume the skills I knew I was always capable of performing. These obstacles allowed me to more fully enjoy the feeling and appreciation of full movement when my body and mind were healed and healthy.

The down times created a greater desire to see what more my body could do than before I was injured physically or mentally. Although it hurt at the time and delayed what I wanted to be doing, I learned to become a better gymnast through all of my sports injuries. This is *The Pendulum*.

The emotions on your own pendulum swing allow you to understand the joy and sorrow of any sport within your range of experience. We need to experience pain to enjoy pleasure. This is a universal law. However, we also get to decide how long we want to experience some of our pain. Sometimes, physical and mental pains are incurable and out of our control. But, some pain is a choice.

Although I believe we must feel many unpleasant things, I also believe you can choose how long you will allow yourself to linger in these unpleasant feelings. Emotions are said to simply be vibrations in the body (energy in motion). Thus, emotions won't physically kill you. How long you choose to *linger,* or allow "these vibrations," is a choice.

Emotions on either side of the Pendulum are your choice. Everyone will experience both sides to a certain extent, but how long you choose to linger on either side of the emotional ride is within your power to control, through your thoughts. We all have free agency; therefore, our thoughts are ours to choose.

Lingering in emotions of self-doubt, insecurities, shame, or fears will cause a self-fulfilling prophecy of failure at the gym. Lingering on the side of confidence, humility, and hope will result in feelings of self-worth and success no matter the circumstance.

The most beautiful part of *The Pendulum* is the joy you get to experience on the other side of the swing. There's always the other side. You get to choose how long you want to linger in the hard, negative, miserable side of the swing in order to get back to the peace, joy, calm side.

Sometimes, it serves you to choose to feel lost, disappointed, afraid, sad, and angry. So, you may indulge in those emotions for a while. You may want someone to feel bad for your situation or the pain you're experiencing. However, as soon as you recognize that you don't have to give in to negative emotions or that you don't have to mirror the emotions of others, then you will find your own personal power.

You now realize that you get to decide how you want to feel, how long you want to feel that way, and what you want to do about those emotions. You are liberated from your own prison of self-inflicted misery.

Gymnasts feel a pressure to perform their very best at all times. This pressure may become overbearing at times and they create scenes in their minds in which they fail. Have you ever entertained similar ideas?

You may have indulged in The Pendulum swing of fear and defeat at some point in your gymnastics activities. This fear of failure and the resulting self-fulfilling prophecy can be a significant problem.

Craig Manning, a sports psychologist, states, "In today's multitasking, text-messaging, highly sophisticated world, the pressure to perform is greater than ever. That being said, when all things are equal...the mentally tough athlete...who has learned to harness the strength of the mind wins every time." (*The Fearless Mind: 5 Essential Steps to Higher Performance,* p. ix)

The pressure to succeed in every area of life seems to have increased in the past years. I am surrounded by parents who ask what they can do to help their athletes do better. I am usually thinking, *Just stay out of their way.* Any type of presence can consciously or unconsciously be interpreted as pressure on an athlete.

It is always the athlete's choice to feel this pressure, but it's still their reality and may affect their performance. Parents usually have only the best intentions for their child and truly want to help. But the athlete will perform, if they're going to perform well, from a more internal commitment to excellence if parents aren't trying to decide what's best in every area of their child's life.

As I've looked back on my life, I've noticed that this Pendulum swing was something that set me apart. I continue to recognize when I'm *choosing* to feel an emotion that doesn't push me to progress or that doesn't contribute to a positive energy. I feel certain this decision to not linger in sorrow or anger for long is due to the habitual routine of bouncing up from constant falls as a gymnast.

Staying down on the ground after a fall doesn't serve any gymnast. A gymnast has the choice to repeatedly linger on the ground, or jump up and try again. You can expect to fall as a part of gymnastics. Knowing that you will fall, you also know that YOU WILL GET BACK UP AGAIN, over and over and over again.

"Again" is one of the most used words heard in a gymnastics facility. You choose to jump up and not stay down and linger in thoughts of self-destruction and "incapable" or negative words. This is your auto-response in the gym. Because most gymnasts are very young, this becomes a neurologically ingrained auto-response to life in general.

You don't linger on the down side of life, but bounce up and move on with the hope that the next move will get you closer to the up-side swing toward perfection of that skill. This is one tool, as a gymnast, for which you can always be grateful. The physical up-down Pendulum swing is part of every gymnastics practice. The emotional Pendulum swing takes a little more awareness to master.

When kid's play video games, they're constantly challenging their avatar to leap over impossible objects or perform difficult tasks. This doesn't seem abnormal in a video game. However, what about in sports? When an obstacle comes before you, do you just hurdle it and move on or does it become a boulder that stops you from progressing?

Sometimes, athletes get injured or have some type of factor that hinders their ability to continue practicing hours a day at their sport. At other times, athletes are perfectly healthy physically; however, their mind is blocking their progression. Decide today that when you face any "obstacle" in your path toward your target, you will change that word to "opportunity."

A roadblock doesn't mean your destination must end, it just requires thinking outside the box. Change the list of "obstacles," "trials," and "difficulties," to "opportunities," "to-do lists," and "new options." Realize the negative emotions that come with disappointments. Don't resist or push those away.

Resisting negative emotions usually heightens their presence. As Carl Jung noted, "What you resist not only persists but will grow in size." If you want something to cease bothering you, then you must give it no attention. If you constantly give your negative thoughts attention, then they will take over. Brooke Castillo, The Life Coach School owner, suggests that your emotions are like little children who constantly ask for attention, but if you give them no attention, they eventually stop.

Therefore, instead of letting those negative emotions take charge in the front seat of your life and decisions, put them in the back seat, and then focus on the emotions you want to enjoy right now. Choose to focus on hope and belief in your abilities to progress as a gymnast. Find ways to create to-do lists when a boulder rolls into your path. Take action.

It's one thing to think about these ideas that are offered and believe them, but it's an entirely new level to try them and experience the possibility that they may work for you.

> *"Most people think more about what they want while doing things that they don't want."*
>
> —*Abraham Hicks.*

Chapter 4 Highlights

- The Pendulum is similar to Newton's Cradle Toy.
- The Pendulum opens your understanding to the fact that whenever you're feeling one emotion, the opposite emotion is also available to choose. When you feel discouraged and defeated in gymnastics, you'll also eventually experience the opposite emotions of confidence and success.
- You get to choose how long you want to linger on either side of the Pendulum swing.
- When gymnastics is hard, eventually it's bound to feel easy again with enough time or mental clarity and choice.
- Recognize that hard times are followed by good times, then you'll be enlightened and inspiring for others.
- Just as the Newton's toy is on a continuum, your emotions regarding your sport will swing on both sides of struggle to success.

- Adversity and taking a chance on yourself are key to personal development.
- Both sides of emotions are inevitable. How long you stay on either side is your choice.

  "Pain is inevitable, suffering is a choice."

  —*Haruki Murakami*

What's Ahead in Chapter 5

Next, you will pull together all the tools of self-improvement to help you reach a higher objective. The following technique is a seamless cyclical routine to cleanse your body and mind, fill them with confidence, then move on to inspiring those around you.

Chapter 4 Action Items

Journal:

1. Write three circumstances you want to feel better about right now.

2. Write the same three circumstances, then add the emotion to those situations as if you have always felt the way you wanted to in #1.

3. Believe #2 is your current reality. It's just a choice.

4. Write a goal you can complete daily.

5. Write a goal that will take you time, hard work, and that stretches your imagination.

5
The Perfect 10.0 Routine

"Champions aren't made in the gyms. Champions are made from something they have deep inside them — a desire, a dream, a vision."

—Muhammad Ali

"That which we **persist in doing becomes easier** to do, not that the nature of the thing has changed but that our power to do has increased."

—Ralph Waldo Emerson

"A person's true character is revealed by what he does when no one is watching."

—John Wooden

CHAPTER 5 TOOLS:

The Perfect 10.0 Formula

The process of putting all the mental, emotional, and physical tools together to implement your individualized elite-level daily routine. This is a simple idea that will create the beautiful athletic life that inspires and generates amazing results.

Clean, Fill, Share

A straightforward pattern to use throughout your athletic day. **Clean** out all aspects of your gymnastics life that add any burden to your day. **Fill** your daily routine carefully and intentionally with things that are inspiring and motivational. Then, **Share** your talent and light with the world to inspire greatness in others.

Gymnasts are constantly reaching for the 10.0 score, or the perfect ten. The fight and effort to reach perfection is real and difficult. Because of this supreme ideal, many gymnast may feel weighed down at times with burdens of inadequacy and defeat.

You may ask yourself if you'll ever be able to perform a 9.0 routine, let alone a 10.0 level of perfection.

The beautiful part about gymnastics is that because perfection is the goal, most gymnasts will never achieve it. That may not sound beautiful, but the fact is that if you're participating in gymnastics only for a 10.0, then you're in the wrong sport. You'll find no fulfillment as a gymnast.

Because nobody will ever achieve perfection in every single routine and every single skill in the optional skills book, everyone can stop stressing about being perfect. This alleviates the fear of never reaching something that is unreachable for now. This allows you to work as hard as you're willing to work, make as many sacrifices as you're willing to sacrifice, and enjoy the movements of every skill as much as you want to enjoy them.

Many coaches ask their gymnasts to write goals for the upcoming competition season. One six-year-old, a kindergartener, was working with her parents to consider possibilities. Eventually, she and her parents decided she should win three out of the four meets in which she was entered. Can you see the problem with this type of goal? What happens when the sweet six-year-old places second or doesn't place at all? What was all her effort for?

The burden of losing sight of your initial love for gymnastics is found in the higher levels of competition as well. When you're a level-8 gymnast and going into your sophomore year at high school, do you decide it's not worth the hours in the gym to hope for a scholarship? Do you quit? Do you justify your choices with the typical, "I'm missing out on social life"? What separates you from your passion for the sport?

Some have felt the burden of not obtaining college scholarships and felt intensely saddened by the waste of many years and finances sacrificed on their behalf. A gymnast may have this intensely damaging belief while forgetting the valuable memories and lessons she has learned in those years along the way.

You must find a way to let go of the ideal perfect 10.0 routine and focus on the perfect 10.0 daily lifestyle. This doesn't allow room for laziness in the gym. Just as when I was a competitive gymnast, I believe that I can reach perfection even today. I'll never lose hope of perfection eventually. I may not **BE** perfect yet, but I strive for perfection in little things daily. Continue to work to perfect individual parts of everything you do, and someday, those parts will add up to something great.

Eventually, we all come to a point where we realize that this life isn't just about us. I used to watch the level 10s during gymnastics when I was eight years old and aspired to be like them someday. They were so pretty, graceful, powerful, and strong. Everything looked easy for them.

As a little girl, my favorite athlete to watch on television was the famous Mary Lou Retton. I even had the haircut and the American flag leotard that all little gymnasts wore at that time. Mary Lou won the gold medal at the Olympics of 1984. Mia Hamm, a nationally recognized soccer player, once said, "Somewhere behind the athlete you've become and the hours of practice and the coaches who have pushed you, is a little girl who fell in love with the game and never looked back...play for her."
Hopefully, we all have someone who inspires us to be

better than we currently are. Along the same lines, realize that someone may be looking to you as their inspiration as well.

The Perfect 10.0 formula has filled my life with light, excellence, and a strong desire to give back because of those who once inspired me and many others and who still do. There are three parts to **the Perfect 10.0 formula:**

Clean: Clean out your body, mind, and emotions. This will relieve much of the burden you carry as a perfectionist and a person striving to obtain a 10.00 score someday.

Fill: Fill your body and mind with anything motivational, inspirational, and *Light.* This will revitalize, energize, and fill you with passion for gymnastics.

Serve: Look for opportunities throughout your day to give back. This will give you a profound sense of continued purpose to your gymnastics career and provide you with valuable leadership qualities. Do something kind for someone else. Share your gymnastics knowledge with a teammate, smile at a lower-level gymnast, and thank your coaches and parents for their help.

CLEAN

Cleansing keeps your mind and body free of unnecessary weight. It doesn't matter whether the weight is physical, mental, or emotional. Anything that causes weight to your "shoulders" needs to be eliminated. You must work to get rid of these unproductive loads if you want to make a difference as an athlete or in any area of your life.

One of the best ways to clean and fill yourself is by what you choose to put into your body. This has a great impact on every other part of your life, especially your productivity during practice.

The Light Plan (detailed in *Flippin' Awesome Gymnast, Vol. II*) is solely a question we ask ourselves whenever we choose what to eat and how much: "Do I feel Light?" Everything we eat increases or decreases our light, or our ability to do what we truly desire. Choose wisely what you put inside your body.

A motivated and productive day begins with a good early morning routine. There is a power in the early mornings. The reason why early morning is effective has to do with the angle of the sun's rays on the Earth's magnetic field.

The sun charges the magnetic field and this affects your pineal gland. The hormones from the pineal gland regulate your circadian rhythms or sleep-wake cycle patterns.

There are theories that the pineal gland senses light similar to the way your eyes sense light. Some Eastern religions call this gland the *third eye* or the *mind's eye*. This *mind's eye* is considered to be like a sixth sense which gives extraordinary insight.

Without a desire to wake early enough to enjoy this secret sauce, you will be missing one of the greatest gifts you could receive every day.

If you choose to start your day with early morning uninterrupted time and a still mind to create what will happen the rest of your day, you'll feel a positive change that you won't want to give away to sleep. That sounds more efficient and enjoyable than waiting for the night to come to plan your day.

I begin my day with meditation, affirmations, and goal reviews. Then I write in my journal to complete my morning *GIFT* (detailed in *Flippin' Awesome Gymnast, Vol. II*). The *GIFT* is an acronym that stands for Gratitude, Inspiration, Feeling, and Thoughtfulness. It's my early morning journal writing method.

When I was a gymnast, I exercised in the afternoon, but today, I choose to get my body moving early. I always wake to a large glass of water and continue to hydrate my body all day. Furthermore, the food I eat is 80% Light foods, which include any food that's produced by the sunlight and provides me energy. This is my morning routine.

During the years that I was a young gymnast, I had gymnastics as a motivation to wake early and complete my list of items in order to be able to focus only on the afternoon workouts. In college, I was lucky to have two wonderful roommates who would wake early with me. We had similar morning routines and supported each other in our personal desire of growth and achievement. It has now been 20 years since I graduated from college, and my routine continues to be similar.

Sleep was on the top of my list of priorities as a competitive gymnast. To this day, my siblings tease me about my sleep needs. When my siblings and I were supposed to wake up at 5:00 am for paper routes in order to pay for my gymnastics lessons, I would ask my sweet dad, "How will I ever get to the Olympics if I don't get enough sleep?" My sister would usually groan at this typical request of mine and then end up doing all my routes with my dad. It was a great way to get an extra hour of sleep.

Years later, at Stanford University, I took a class from Dr. William Dement, a leading authority on sleep. In one lecture, he taught the importance of getting 8 hours plus or minus 15 minutes of sleep for every adult. The consequences were considerable whether you chose enough or not enough sleep. Choosing to be sleep deprived would cause unconscious negative results.

Some use caffeine to re-energize; I choose naps. Afternoon 15-20-minute power naps were an essential part of my athletic days, and continue to give me the afternoon lift, energy, and clarity I need to continue on my path of an intentional and mentally aware day. Power napping takes practice, just like everything else. For most of us, relaxing our body and mind quickly enough to make a 15-minute nap useful, requires the ability to release distractions and relax. (refer to the *Tension-Relaxation* tool in Volume I)

At night, I would repeat this routine of meditation, inspiration, and journal writing. I found that I needed to record any inspiration I received in the morning and make goals for my workouts, then hold myself accountable in the evening journal time as to how my day actually played out.

This routine was my "all-around" cleanser. Just like you must be a great "All-Around Gymnast," including beam, floor, vault, and bars, in order to become an elite gymnast, you must also take care to clean all areas of your of life. The Stanford Women's Gymnastics Team coaches, administrative staff, nutritionist, weight coach, and sports psychologist provided constant help in the cleaning process.

When I didn't know what was best for me in these areas of my life, I had the resources listed above readily available to fill in the gaps. Elite athletes typically rely on these types of resources to help with the cleansing process throughout their days.

FILL

Fill is the process of being intentional and aware of what you will and won't put in your body and mind, knowing that those choices will impact your ability to perform, feel peace, and share your talents during your day.

The word **Fill** can be replaced with **Feel** because the two words are synonymous in the context of this athletic tool. Filling includes similar aspects to the *Clean* process. Once you *clean* your mind, body, and emotions, then those same choices will fill you up with energy, knowledge, light, inspiration, and direction.

If you **Fill** your mind and body with poor choices, you'll **Feel** weighed down and tired, disappointed and confused, worthless and depressed. Conversely, if you *Fill* your mind with light, you'll *Feel* enlightened. *Filling* is just as important as *Cleaning*. You cannot move to the next step of *Serving* without properly filling yourself up. My favorite part of every day is the process of *Cleaning* and *Filling* during my GIFT journaling time. I'm usually focused and ready to *Serve* once my daily GIFT is recognized.

It's like a garden. You get rid of the weeds in the cleaning process, and then you fill your garden with flowers or vegetation. *Cleaning* takes the "weight off your shoulders" while *Filling* increases your desire, self-motivation, determination, to be able to focus on what you want. If you don't know what you want, then *Filling* is going to be a waste of time because it has no purpose.

If you spend the time weeding your garden, but don't fill it with something beautiful or productive, what happens? The weeds return or try to return. So, if you don't intentionally *Fill* your garden, or replace the weeds with flowers, vegetables, or fruits, then either you have barren ground or weeds will return. That's the perfect example of living a life in the past. And that's okay. There is no judgement. You get to choose your level of gymnastics success.

Worry is a weed, fear is a weed, and anxiety is a weed. These are all past or future ideas that have no foundation. Our species is the only species that can create in our mind, a circumstance that is not founded upon reality. We can experience stress that has no true basis, even to the point of physical and emotional detriment when, in fact, the worrisome circumstance has never actually even occurred in real life. We create our reality in our mind before we experience it.

Dr. Sapolsky of Stanford University has written a book called, *Why Don't Zebras Get Ulcers*. In it, he explains that animals normally respond and are hard-wired in their brains to respond to actual stimuli, not made up stimuli. Our reality is our own reality. In other words, we believe it, so it becomes true to us. Sometimes, it's a made-up reality without a foundation.

A weed can appear as a beautiful flower. My daughter, Mikayla, used to pick large, yellow dandelions before they died and turned white. She would come in with arms full of these "beautiful" weeds. They grew to be great in size and for as often as she would pick them, there would always be many more to be picked.

 It can be overwhelming, but as you work on one little part of your mental, physical, and emotional gardens, you will find that replacing them or filling them with flowers will eventually provide you with a garden of intentional plants instead of weeds. It doesn't mean the weeds are gone forever. This is why *Cleansing, Filling, and Serving* is a continual process.

In daily life, from the music we listen to, the books we read, the shows we watch, etc., we are constantly impacting our *cleansing* and *filling* abilities. Journaling is essential to this process where you can *free write* all your thoughts and goals, repent, choose to make small changes regularly, and come to see who you are in the process. Cleansing and filling is a constant cycle throughout the day, not just a one-time early morning event.

Serve

Serving is what many people are eventually inclined to do by contributing to society and giving back for all they've been given. **Serving** others without first taking care of your own needs will burn you out.

When you haven't carefully planned your own time and space to continually feel relieved of burdens through cleaning and filling yourself up with things that bring light and joy into your life, then you're giving to others from an empty, messy place. What you're giving to others from an unclean, unfilled place is corrupt, cynical, critical, burdensome, or from a feeling of obligation instead of love.

You can only maintain this kind of service for a short period before you'll want to give up or give in. *Serving* from a place of love comes with pure intentions, desires, and increases your energy and light. Energy is a natural result of *serving* from a healthy space. As you encourage teammates and appreciate coaches, you'll feel a sense of contentment that's different from sticking ten beam skills in a row.

In athletics, you work hard to excel in different areas in order to show your skills. Some athletes don't enjoy performing; however, that's part of any sport. The audience is enjoying the entertainment as well as the dedication a person has taken to excel in that area of their life. The performance or competition is also *Serving*. It's sharing what you've learned and developed to allow others to enjoy as well as yourself.

If there was never any *Service* with athletics, I believe the enjoyment would significantly decrease. Athletes, in general, like to show what they've worked so hard to create. It's just like an artist who shows a painting, a pianist who performs in a recital, or a writer who publishes their work.

We all have some innate desire to share what we do with others. We all want to think it blesses another's life because of what we've accomplished. We all want to *be a part of* something greater than ourselves. In the end, once you decide that helping others is important along your own road to gymnastics fulfillment, then something changes inside of you. Remember, what you want and why you really want it changes your little daily decisions. You'll be looking for reasons to give the love you've filled yourself with to another.

As I pondered the lessons learned from my athletic career, I remembered how I didn't use this *Clean, Fill, Serve* tool well at times. I recall participating at a meet in my home state of Arizona my senior year in college. I had a daily *Perfect 10.0 routine* that I kept very well in general. I knew what food to eat the day of a competition for my best physical energy level. I chose, however, to go out to a restaurant with my fiancé and future mother-in-law the day of the Arizona meet.

I ordered a meal that I had never eaten before and ate more than I should have. I had a lump in my side the entire meet, fell three times from beam, and made huge mistakes on bars and a large step to the side on my vault. I had never in my gymnastics career experienced a competition like that. I knew the entire time that no matter where I was mentally, I hadn't cleansed or filled my body the way I needed to in order to perform optimally.

My skills were great, my mind was great, but my body wasn't. I had made a choice and it negatively affected me and my team's results. I wasn't able to *Serve* my team at that particular meet because I hadn't prepared properly. Everything we choose to do has seen and unseen impacts on the lives of those around us and on our own life. When we keep a tight daily routine, we're Serving in the most efficient manner possible for us in our personal classroom of everyday life.

I must admit that *Serving* wasn't something that I focused on much during my years of competitive gymnastics. I was too concerned about my own time and my own abilities. I didn't focus on others in a way that I currently do.

Gratitude was part of my life. I wouldn't leave a workout without saying thank you to coaches, athletic trainers, or anyone who was around and helping. But, it wasn't until I opened my own gym and helped choreograph and coach that I realized the enjoyment of *Serv*ing others in a more impactful way. Some of my favorite memories now are offering help to those who are current gymnasts who are trying to succeed.

The *Clean, Fill, Serve* method adapts and adjusts as needed. Even though I didn't define it in those terms when I was competitive, I had to make choices daily that would clear my body, mind, and emotions in order to fill those parts of me with positive, energetic and wise elements. By emptying areas of your mind through journaling in the morning, throughout the day, and then re-evaluating this process before bed, you allow yourself to choose that with which you'll be filled.

There are times in my life when I've felt like a bumblebee. Jackson Brown once said, "Go for it! Take a chance. There are times you must trust that silent voice inside you. According to the laws of aerodynamics the bumblebee cannot fly. I guess no one bothered to tell the bee. Keep flying!" Somebody forgot to tell me that I wasn't supposed to be able to fly.

When I was a junior in high school, Coach Lisa Spini asked me to talk with her in her office. I remember this meeting as if it were yesterday. Lisa's first question was, "You've kept your grades up right?" "Yes," I replied. She continued on to inform me that Stanford University wanted to recruit me. My first questions were, "Where is Stanford University? What state is it in? Is it a good school?"

I spent the next few months visiting a variety of universities, struggling with where I felt I was to attend. I had always assumed I would attend ASU, as John Spini had been the head coach there as well as a coach at AZ Twisters periodically. However, what I see in hindsight is that my daily choices had led me on a path that I wasn't aware I was choosing.

One student at our high school diligently worked to go to Stanford University, weighing every decision in terms of whether that class or this club would somehow get him there. He didn't get into Stanford. I've thought of this student often and haven't understood the results clearly. I definitely didn't have Stanford on my radar as a future college choice.

Every time I think of that singular opportunity, my heart swells with gratitude. I often wonder why I was blessed with such an opportunity. Tears fill my eyes when I talk of those few years at that prestigious college. In the first couple of weeks of attending college, I called my dad and said, "What am I thinking? I can never make it through this place. I'm not smart enough."

But, with encouragement from my parents, teammates, and roommates as well as the resources provided, my confidence grew and I did learn, enjoy, and complete my degree at Stanford University.

Now, what am I supposed to do with the knowledge and experience I've received in order to help others? My *Perfect 10.0 Routine* of *Cleaning, Filling, and Serving* at school and gymnastics has led me to experiences that I didn't know I could have even hoped for. As you write goals and develop your own *Perfect 10.0 Routine*, I'm confident that you'll enjoy more beautiful experiences than you would ever think to consider in your journal.

Knowing what you choose to **Fill** your mind and body with will have a direct impact on your day, your workouts, your relationships, and your life. How you **Feel** in each area of your life will inspire greatness or doubt. Overall, choose carefully what you'll allow to fill your life, your time, your desires, your thoughts, and your actions.

Once you feel physically fueled, mentally capable, and emotionally calm, then *Serve* in a controlled manner. Try to have a positive impact on the world around you. The joy of life comes in the *Serving* after the hard work of *Cleaning and Filling*. Service and contribution ignites and calms something inside and lifts your spirit.

Cleaning, Filling, then *Serving* is the pattern of life that leads to fullness and love. What you're becoming is more important than what you're accomplishing. Take the small steps each day to keep progressing toward your personalized *Perfect 10.0 Routine*. Choose to be an inspiring and **Flippin' Awesome Gymnast!**

The Perfect Elite Level 10.0 Routine for Me:

I am going to share my daily routine, but you must create one that fits you. This daily routine can change and morph to fit changing situations. As an athlete, I used to decide how to make my body and mind be tighter, faster, and more consistent. I currently use this tool of The Perfect 10.00 Routine, which includes the *Clean, Fill, Serve* method, to make my days more meaningful, inspired, and productive.

Side Note:

Volumes I & II of the *Flippin' Awesome Gymnast* book series includes many other tools that I'll briefly mention, which are in my own personal *Perfect 10.0* daily routine of *Clean, Fill, Serve*. Read those volumes to find out more about these and other tips, including how to eliminate fears in the *Blast Off Sequence*, find your personal *Range*, use the *Tension-Relaxation* technique, create your *Cue Words,* post your *Mind Guard,* play the *Brain Game*, utilize the *CTFAR formula*, choose the *Light Plan*, enjoy *Calming* techniques, and see your gymnastics *Vision* of success.

The Morning Routine=
    a. Large glass of water
    b. Meditation
    c. Journaling The GIFT, including Affirmations, Vision Board, & Goal Review
    d. Exercise & Stretch
    e. Use the Light Plan

The Day Routine=
    a. Quick Breathing tool

b. Cue Words & The Mind Guard

c. Power Nap (if needed)

d. Drink water all day

e. Cleanse, Fill, Serve all day

The Night Routine=

a. Glass of water

b. Meditate

c. Journal: Review & Accountability to yourself

d. Tension-Relaxation Technique

e. Visualization

f. Sleep 8 hours (+/- 15 minutes)

Chapter 5 Highlights

- The Perfect 10.0 Routine: The Routine that brings all aspects of an elite-level daily routine together, specialized just for you. It includes the *Clean, Fill, Serve* method.

- **Clean, Fill, Serve Method** is the daily routine created to **Clean** all aspects of your life in order to **Fill** your life carefully and intentionally with energy, focus, and light. Then **Serve** your love for gymnastics to the world, inspiring greatness in your teammates, coaches, gym, and others.

- The three parts of the *Clean, Fill, Serve* method have a continual cycle of crossover and cross-checking that develop meaningful habits.

- *CLEAN* your emotional, mental, and physical life to get rid of excess weight.

- *FILL* yourself with dreams, energy, motivational, and inspiration elements in order to thrive in the gym every day.

- You're then ready to *SERVE* by using your talents and abilities from a healthy space and with energy to lift and help other aspiring gymnasts around you.

- If you *SERVE* without taking the proper steps to *CLEAN* and *FILL* yourself first, then you will become exhausted, resentful, jealous, and depleted.
- *Serving* will bring you more satisfaction than all your years of being a competitive gymnastics.
- Be inspired, then go inspire.
- Be a **Flippin' Awesome Gymnast** for others to emulate.

What's Ahead in Chapter Worksheets

As you implement the chapter tools incorporated into these worksheets, you'll discover more desire, purpose, and commitment to becoming an inspiring gymnast. See how to take the methods discussed and put them into action by completing the worksheets provided.

Chapter 5 Action Items

Challenge:

1. Wake up 1 hour before the rest of your house.
2. Give yourself *The GIFT* of a quiet morning and see where your thoughts and choices lead that day through the *Cleanse, Fill, Serve* method or, in other words, *The Perfect 10.0 Routine*.

APPENDIX I

CHAPTER WORKSHEETS

Chapter 1: Sweet Spot

Journal:

1. How can you be bold and stand out from other gymnasts?

_____

_____

2. What sets you apart from your competitors at a meet?

_____

_____

3. Why should a judge give you a higher score than another gymnast?

_____

_____

4. Why do you think you are special?

_____

_____

5. How can you be a leader in your gym?

_____

_____

6. How will your confidence help your teammates
   succeed?

_____

_____

Chapter 2: Words You Never Say

1. Get two boxes (like empty shoe boxes or tissue boxes). On one, write your own name; on the other box, write the word *Universe*. When you're frustrated and feel that you're not progressing, write those obstacles that are hindering you on paper and divide them into each box. Put those things that you can change in the first box. Put those things you cannot change in the Universe box and let them go.

2. Today I felt like saying "I can't," but, instead, I said,

   "_____"

3. Today I felt like saying, "I already know that," but, instead, I said,

   "_____"

Chapter 3: Power Phrase

Challenge:

1. Make a greater effort to say "thank you" throughout the day to anyone who helps you.
2. Start every morning by writing 1-10 things for which you're grateful.

   a. _____

   b. _____

   c. _____

   d. _____

   e. _____

   f. _____

   g. _____

   h. _____

   i. _____

   j. _____

Chapter 4: The Pendulum

Journal:

1. Write three circumstances you want to feel better about right now at gym.

    a. _____

    _____

    b. _____

    _____

    c. _____

    _____

2. Write the same three circumstances, then add the desired emotion to those situations as if you've always felt the way you wanted to in #1.

    a. _____

    _____

    b. _____

    _____

    c. _____

    _____

3. Believe #2 is your current reality. It's just a choice.

Chapter 5: Clean, Fill, Serve

1. Today, I cleansed my body, mind, and emotions when I:

   _____

   _____

   _____

   _____

   _____

2. I chose to feel _____when I did this.

3. Today, I Filled my body, mind, and emotions when I:

   _____

   _____

   _____

   _____

   _____

4. I chose to feel _____when I did this.

5. Today, I Served as I:

_____

_____

_____

_____

_____

6. I chose to feel_____ when I
   did this.

APPENDIX II

STRONG MIND WORKSHEET

- As you lift others in the gym, and in all areas of your life, you'll find an enhanced sense of purpose and enjoyment in your own workouts and athletic career.

1. What do I want to become as a gymnast?

   _____

   _____

   _____

2. Why do I want to become this?

   _____

   _____

   _____

3. How can I align my mind, body, and emotions to reach my own person sweet spot?

   _____

   _____

   _____

4. How can I make someone else's day easier at gym today?

_____

_____

_____

5. When I feel like saying negative phrases, I will ask myself what I am afraid of and write it down:

_____

_____

_____

6. How can I show gratitude for gymnastics in my life?

_____

_____

_____

7. When I feel like quitting, I will recognize that the other side of the Pendulum is also present. Today, despite my circumstance, I chose to feel:

_____

_____

_____

8. I choose to live the Perfect 10.0 life of Clean, Fill, Serve by:

_____

_____

_____

9. My own personal daily elite-level routine includes the following:

_____

_____

_____

CONGRATULATIONS AND THANK YOU FOR
READING THIS BOOK; WORKING TO
BECOME AN INSPIRING GYMNAST!

About the Author

Amy Twiggs is a wife and a mother of four teenagers. She is a former elite gymnast and, in 1993, she was a member of the developmental National Women's Gymnastics Team. She received a full-ride athletic scholarship for gymnastics from Stanford University where she obtained a Bachelor's Degree in Psychology with a focus in Health & Development. Mental Training is her passion. Amy's education has provided many opportunities for her to give back to athletes. She has coached and choreographed for 25 years at a variety of gymnastics facilities. She is a former USAG Judge and currently owns the Flippin' Awesome Gymnastics facility in St. George, Utah.

If you are interested in contacting Amy Twiggs please email her at
flippinawesomecoaching@gmail.com

Made in the USA
Middletown, DE
11 November 2021